MEL BAY PRESENTS

A Renaissance Christmas

7 GUITAR SOLOS ON RENAISSANCE CHRISTMAS CLASSICS

BY JAMES KALAL

CD CONTENTS

1. Lullay My Liking [2:16]
2. O Come, O Come Emmanuel/Ensemble & Solo [6:28]
3. Ding Dong Merrily On High [1:15]
4. Deck the Halls [1:16]
5. Coventry Carol [1:25]
6. What Child is This/Greensleeves [7:38]
7. Lo' How a Rose E're Blooming [1:13]

Pages 30 and 31 are left blank intentionally.

Visit us on the Web at www.melbay.com — E-mail us at email@melbay.com

Table of Contents

Foreword

The music selected for this book seems to lift you gently back to by-gone days to an era more leisurely paced than our own. We sincerely hope you enjoy *A Renaissance Christmas*. I have really enjoyed the collaborative effort with my friend-associate, Robert W. Fraser, of creating a new Renaissance project that would focus first and foremost on early Christmas music and would include appropriate cover art, biblical text and poetry dating from this exciting period. We hoped to achieve a play list that would be very festive to listen to and would also provide arrangements ranging from the traditional "easier to learn" lute solos to more advanced settings with today's harmonies. Each piece is cloaked in the special beauty and warmth that is characteristic of the guitar. We hope you enjoy the added dimension of a "mix and match" approach in the myriad arrangements presented. For example, *What Child is This/Greensleeves* begins with an olden lute version followed by interludes that segue into other sections.

Historical Notes

Gregorian chant from the 12th century has found a new popularity in this decade with a group of Benedictine monks from Santa Domingo de Silos, Spain. *Lullay My Liking* is a "telling" English setting that is very easy to learn. The arrangement is based on simple chant similar to the Gregorian type. *O Come, O Come Emmanuel* also has early "chant-plainsong" characteristics in thc arrangement. There were eight church modes employed for composing chant as follows: Dorian, Phrygian, Hypophrygian, Lydian, Hypolydian, and Mixolydian.

I have a special interest in the English poetry of Chaucer because it helped me better understand the early composers who wrote for the lute and the period of history they lived in. English poetry evolved and was intertwined in its development with the spread of hymns. It developed from the homiletic verse, the metrical chronicle and the melancholy elegiac poetry into metrical romance. Chaucer employed an Italian humanism in his new demonstration of the possibilities of verse. It's interesting to note a marked growth of the democratic spirit in the 1300's and religious literature written for the common man. This democratic spirit lead to the spread of hymns through the activity of famous preaching friars that we associate with Chaucer. I especially liked the *Nun's Priest Tale* from the *Canterbury Tales* which refers to a pilgrimage of friars as was so popular at that time. Only in the lifetime of Chaucer are there signs of the carols beginning to emerge as something different from a poem. It is difficult if not impossible to find any example of an authentic carol with certainty to be dated earlier than 1400. (Chaucer's Roundel of c. 1382, No. 128 has to be arranged in order to be sung as a carol.)

As Joseph was a-walking,
He heard an angel sing:
"This night shall be born
Our heavenly King."

He neither shall be born
In housen nor in hall,
Nor in the place of Paradise,
But in an ox's stall.

He neither shall be clothed
In purple nor in pall,
But all in fair linen
As wear baby's all.

He neither shall be rocked
In silver nor in gold,
But in a wooden cradle
that rocks on the mould.

He neither shall be christened
In white wine nor red,
But with fair spring water

Lullay My Liking

D.C. al Fine

7

O Come, O Come Emmanuel

Traditional 13th century plainsong

arranged by E. James Kalal
and Robert W. Fraser

Modern Version I

Ding Dong Merrily On High

Deck the Halls

arranged by E. James Kalal
and Robert W. Fraser

Coventry Carol

arranged by E. James Kalal
and Robert W. Fraser

What Child Is This?

Introduction

Greensleeves

Anon.
arranged by E. James Kalal

Interlude 2

18

Out of your slepe arise and wake,
For God mankind now hath itake
All of a maide without any make;
Of all women she berethe the belle
Nowel.

And throwe a maide faire and wis
Now man is made of full grete pris;
Now angeles knelen to manes servis;
And at this time all this bifel.
Nowel.

Now man is brighter than the sonne;
Now man is heven an hie shall (wonne);
Blessed be God this game is begonne
And his moder emperesse of helle
Nowel.

Interlude 4

Interlude 5

Finale

He's seen, He's seen! why then a round,
Let's kiss the sweet and holy ground;
And all rejoice that we have found
A King before conception crown'd.

Come then, come then, and let us bring
Unto our pretty Twelfth-tide King,
Each one his several offering;

And when night comes we'll give Him wassailing;
And that His treble honours may be seen,
We'll chose Him King, and make His mother
Queen.

Modern Version

Prelude

Lo' How A Rose E'er Blooming

arranged by Robert W. Fraser

EXCELLENCE IN MUSIC